NATALIE SOMMER

SCRIBE ARTIST

& STORYISM

A - Z

50 FOR 50

Contents - Scribe Art Pieces

Contents - Scribe Art Pieces (continued)

Foreword

"Natalie is a truly exceptional person, deeply spiritual, with a big heart, depths of humour and compassion, the capacity to shine bright, an innate ability to relate to others.

Natalie's poetry and art reflect her vibrancy, energy and tension. Each work stands alone; and each work gives insight to an effervescent whole."

Rabbi Jeremy Lawrence is Senior Rabbi at Finchley United Synagogue, where Natalie has run children's services for 12 years.

He has previously served at The Great Synagogue, Sydney, Australia and the Auckland Hebrew Congregation, New Zealand.

His interests include interfaith dialogue and computer animation.

"Natalie makes positivity seem effortless in her storyism as a Scribe Artist.

Optimism is a catalyst for the extraordinary and from which only good things can happen.

Natalie etches creativity in all she does with a great outlook on life we can all learn from".

Cllr.Eva Greenspan
Mayor of Barnet 2006/2007
Liveryman of the worshipful company of artscholars and the worshipful company of musicians.

Foreword

"Natalie's scribe art is colourful, noisy, vibrant, vivacious and larger than life - just like her personality.

This is what she penned for me to mark our friendship."

"Roses are dull, and so predictably red
Violets keep growing that insipid blue
OUR landlines painted social media itself
When scribe artist me met pop artist YOU!"

When The Cynthia Corbett Gallery hosted her first solo show, art critic Estelle Lovatt proclaimed that "America has Lichtenstein, we have Azzopardi", a statement that Azzopardi regards as "a wonderful compliment".

Deborah Azzopardi outside her studio, 2014.
Photo by Christna Schek

"The art of storytelling is as old as the first human experience. Natalie Sommer's scribe art and storyism is a passionate, wonderful gift for conjuring up the imagination.

Her work is visceral, honest, joyful, sad, real and raw. In this world of unrelenting technology, her words and pictures are a breath of fresh air."

Hannah Good grew up without the distraction of television, observing her mum, renowned potter Kate Good. Kate now has over 50 years experience in her field.

Her creativity has been passed to Hannah and her daughter and jeweller Ela. Ladytree Designs and Kate Good pottery are 3 generations of independent and highly skilled women creating beautiful and sustainable items that will succeed time.

Introduction

As a scribe artist my non-conformist mind is intent on painting my take on life and telling each story piece, my storyism.

I am an eschatological scribe, painting for the survival of mankind and my own, my work is enigmatic and the avenues of my poetry often intentionally unfathomable at first glance.

The canvass is written in my heart, reality is distorted and the poem is an intellectual snapshot of the jigsaw experience of the raw pain icons of my mind.

Historically I associate myself with the Pharisees and Scribes referred to in the New Testament (the ancestors of the Rabbinical family I originate from) merging my ancient background within the Old Testament to my secularist modernity and I am painting for my own survival.

With my scribe artist temperament I juggle my identity as a Modern Orthodox Jew, within a passionately pluralistic, multi-cultural mind-set and as a single mother to a mixed race daughter.

My art demonstrates that in the present day I am an authentic Jewish record keeper, passionate about education and liberal thinking. The scribe artist is always tasked with creating something from nothing like a writer creating a new story line.

My work embraces the complex and conflicting psyche of faith's dictates within my ancient Hebrew tradition with references to the Old and New Testaments, written and Oral Law, all faiths and none.

Introduction

Most of my scribe artist pieces would work at any angle and cannot be defined easily.

Seated at my folding table as a scribe artist must, the themes of the canvass must be the universality of what mankind is capable of achieving at its best and at its worst.

The trigger for each scribe artist piece is a real and raw life experience.

I enjoy challenging and articulating the issues we face head on without self-entitlement, whether tortured or not, often with humour and always with a touch of the unexpected.

Scribe artist themes are unlimited; illness, lifestyle choices, addiction, corruption death, bereavement, hamartia of the stranger or inevitably my own, the perilous fragility of the human and animal world to the unparalleled happiness of joy and birth, the ultimate positivity of meaningful success.

Scribe art always remembers kindness is not weakness it is strength.

The art and poetry transforms sphinx like across the canvass and page into the unparalleled and often unusual thought provoking beauty of truth with positive reinforcement as optimism's key.

There is a spirituality within my work as a scribe artist with plays on metaphors, symbols, wording and the importance of colour and what it represents within the context of the canvass and poem to generate a pivotal reaction.

Scribe artists must always be ready to challenge man made interpretations and fight for the ethics and integrity of their work.

ADULT CHILD 08/05/07

No war - no terror
No Holocaust pain -
But for an adult child
So hard to keep positive and sane…

Optimism unlocks insecurities key
First aid kit fits tenacity and overrides depression's key
Life's future gift is all about emotional survival -
So resist at any cost your self-destructive rival…

No one can or should take away
The icons of injustice you never wished to receive
But adult child - mindfulness be assured
Your private traumas we don't know but believe…

Tis fair to say -
Keep those demons at bay….
So why no life still adult child?
"Cos it's wild to be an adult child…"

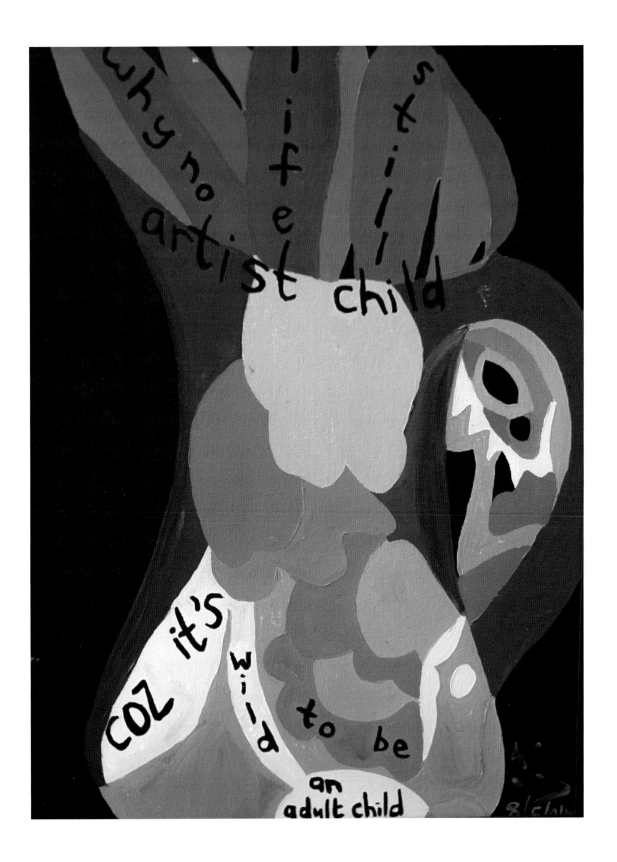

BACK TO FRONT 16/08/08

Is it purely your affront?
Why should I bear the brunt?
Coz you are back to front
In your own solitary witch hunt...

Who said I should
Conform to your insane norm...
When we artists and musicians
Must needs perform...

I am the eternal non-conformist.
Nope, don't want to be kissed
By the control freak
Raging in your midst...

My personality? Won't curb it...
You just want to usurp it...
Burp and swallow, go girl go -
Kicking those down - you are the lowest of the low...

Mean and keen
You aim and fire,
Love handles queen -
I ain't your gun for hire-

True friendship is free
But yours is an autonomy...
You want control?
Cos someone mislaid your soul...

Dark child.
You are not meek and mild
And your freaky lunacy is not my style...

Let go of me - not my love,
Your ego gets a well-deserved shove,
It sure is pretty scenic
When your black pride is really anaemic.

Back

Front

16/8/08

BASKETBALL 18/08/04

Basketball
D'ya recall
Lost ball/
Birth control?

Hey playa,
Balling us all...
Come to the crunch -
D'ya have the gall?

Too proud, shit falls,
You end up with no balls...
Just feelings like brick walls ...
Pretending no duty calls...

Best sperm in the net
You let go of yet...
You try so hard to forget
You aint got no regret....

So yeah - Thy kingdom come.
But whose will be done?
Basketball scored your goal.
Hit - female acacia white soul...
Threw me single motherhood...
You don't want it but should.

So baby child, don't want him back,
Coz you young, gifted and best of all black.

BENEFITS 18/04/04

Idiosyncrasies in 1 instalment,
Lies in a Kabbalistic batch of 4 -
Stable's left 2 pay sane rent!
Hoarse heart-Jewish folklore....

Dreams, pure and unattainable -
Sex, leapfrog, roll and sigh -
Zion rocket, oxymoron fable -
Race black 2 stamp cheque,
Spit 1 white noise out + fly ...

Learning curve -
Bend over and serve!

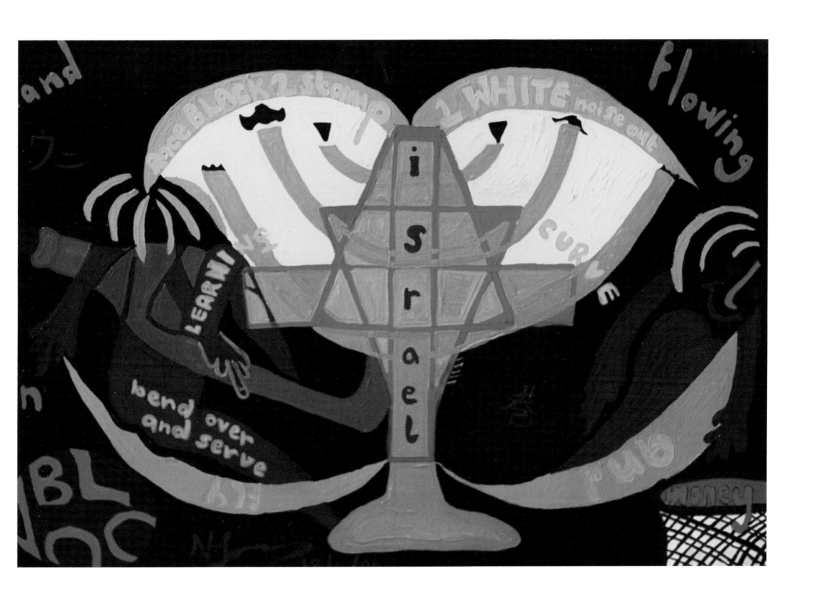

BE POSITIVE 25/02/08

Self-esteem is great with my demon ghosts,
They get to outperform my mind's hosts -
Dancing around to my spirit's lyric,
Pretending victory is not pyrrhic.
We are humble and buoyant
Without the soothsayer and clairvoyant-
And today my soul is fed well
On this 1930's music disc-swell!

Feet first, tap into mindful, nostalgic background.
Positive reinforcement wraps me kindly in the
Sound.
I am healed so don't trip on my egg shell fragility,
And don't drown as I gulp down my own ability..

My adult child grows in a world of souls
Ever present and tangible in my cereal bowls.

I love life and unlike others
Choose not to see hell under the covers.
Don't live in pregnant fear of my precinct
And won't give birth to self-destructive instinct.

Identity crisis is no more than toast and marmite
Tangy emotion - black and white dynamite…

Larger than life, what a laugh
If you dared to worship that Golden Calf -
Reward and punishment hot and smelly,
She was God's baby came out of my belly…

Short intervention - this world fleeting - is it cruel?
Before I get reincarnated in the world to come's
Secondary school.

Does it jar when you stand out more?
Hell -1 did not start this prejudice or war?
So overwhelming the emotion of love
My first aid kit, positive, timeless glove…

Are you a player or another poet?
So what if you are dysfunctional and know it!
Self-esteem is a costume but you must make it fit
If you are to get by life and survive it…

19

BEST BUD BENEVOLENCE 25/08/10

Coloured you in - my Grand Alderman of benevolence
Orange blood war, my ex-soldier never had malevolence
Locked into life's tours, RAOB shades of conscience
Interesting bottle green, crimson blue state of resemblance
Next to 42 from 17 you embraced hell in our defence

The flute and bugle, dead Diana icons give you congruence
Happy 1998, best drummer and Cutler's sword essence
Abstract and indispensable, navy and old gold pretence
Nice Regimental colours, we salute the souls of absence
Killed for Elizabeth Regina in the value of equivalence....

You give every Chelsea Pensioner beauty and credence
Orange William and Catherine of Briganza's affluence
U saved me in your orange - my best bud benevolence....

BIO 13/04/18

Prepare a short bio/personal statement for Natalie Sommer?
My first non-conformist response must be why bother?
But artistic work ethic meets keen service provider
And broad experience and understanding makes me wiser....

From GCSE in art where I could act my pieces on paper
To Willesden Interior Design College "Mother loves her idiotic son" caper....
"You have a style there", they said - "Stark, determined bold" -
My art pain is different to the others at 18 years old....

Self-taught addiction paints the birth of my own brand - "storyism"
I am now born artist and poet - cradle my take on life in rhythm
Feast or famine generates in the art world
So my canvasses and poems till now were on hold ....

Single parent to a mixed race larger than life 19 year old
Black, white and Jewish - thanks to Kinloss, no soul sold
Senior management 6 days each week helped pay the rent
And on the Sabbath Day, Children's Service Educator is still well spent

I am passionate about education, proud yet pluralistic of my heritage
My work may shout out my Judaism, multicultural love not mute in its message
Love of humanity, reliving the raw emotions of mankind
Painting often from my pain icon - jigsaw snapshots of my mind....

Distortion of reality, truth's beauty is always there
Even if it is unusual - I don't mind if you choose to stare...
Take a chance on my stories painted and written in my heart
Then perhaps buy one or two to make your own "storyism" start......

23

BREASTS AND LEGS 16/09/91

Tikvah - all-pervading Israeli hope
Masquerading - no need for dope
My Yemenite psychic friend
Could drive me round the bend

Instead they pay her to wonder
I sunbathe and paint and ponder
The magic feel better attitude
A pack of divinity cards can exude
Guess what? I am beautifully dysfunctional
And born to paint my story illogical

Firm and resolute pencil and charcoal
Tis true - you may never be an Andy Warhol
But satisfaction and inner peace reign supreme
Fist grasps my angels as I dare draw to dream

Connecting artistic freedom and my critics
With semantics and Semitics
I am forever full of promise
And will conjure up artistic solace
Within the sketches of my comfort zone
Cocktails for my future paintings are sewn

Breasts to tease so someone must needs miss
Legs to wax so someone must needs kiss
Toenails and pedicures so someone must needs trim
I yearn for love yet art must needs seduce him....

CHAMPAGNE SHOE 06/10/91

Fashion by Christian Dior
Stilettoes by Marie Claire
Parisian paupers snatch
Bin food scraps!
But only my solitary friend
"Indifference"
Seems to care....

Beautiful imaginary girl in Paris
Draped over life's chair
Hair long, flowing and gratuitous
At success do you gawk and stare?

Whatever lies ahead for you & me?
Sex? Drugs? University?

Will I ever see you sober again?
In my collection of life pain?

What sleeps ahead?
In our glorious bed?

Sex? Drugs? University?
Single purpose? Wedding trinity?

Will I ever see you inebriated again?
In my collection of art's true gain?

Champagne shoe
Muse of glue
Thoughts & words of gratitude
Soulful fodder of painter's food....

Three cheers to my loving soul
Never let go till we reach our goal.

Will I ever see you dear heart again?
Pumping out colours in my
painting's refrain.

N Summer 6/10/91

CHLOË 01/08/02

Precious gift of godliness.
Miniature giant of love!
Jonah and the whale
Within the belly of karma.
Heartburn of all time.

Swelling of truth
Catapulted into life!
Criss cross-stitches
Gaping change...

Carrying you through
Bureaucracy and pain.
My expression of endurance?
The labour of my life?

Feelings become vacant,
My eyes meeting yours....
"Mummy's baby"!
Her very own scarlet letter...

Nerve racking chords
Melt solitude Into divides of parentage,
"Cry, baby, cry..."

My life becomes another's;
My hopes photosynthesized...
My one now two.
Motherhood; you and me!

Poem Continued Overleaf

Bitter sweet pangs of love,
Newfound almond strength,
Nipple bound dependant
Independence...

Suckling virtue of dilemma.
Loveliness in a gurgle,
Nostalgia's memory riveted
In your smile...

Bottle-fed dreams anew.
Resting on a nap...
Identities shipwrecked;
Absent present
Domesticity, never, never.

Tears mean moments
Locked into chasms of truth.
Acceptance is the keyword
To single mothers...

Don't fight the labour pains
After birth,
They will last as long
As your child does!
Tokens of motherhood.

Sweet Chloë,
My life is in your hands.
Gentle with my love.
Your only constant...

Poem Continued Overleaf

Forgive the father
Knowing not what
He is
Nor what he has
Neither never will he be!

God our heavenly father.
We shall have that rather!
The sharpener
To heart's intellect.

Every tear you shed
Has His name inscribed,
And your mother's undying love,
Escorting you there, wherever.

For never never land
Is not ours to see
Nor ours to question,
It is ours to live...

Your DNA blueprint,
Your blood, my albatross...
Black as thunder
Is the voice of God!

I thank him for you.
And forgive.
Pebbles on the shore...
We are all made in His image?
Amen

CHLOË-CHAI-18 24/11/17

My jewel, my prize, the love of my life -
Your choice, your parent, the daughter not the wife...
My dreams, my hopes, the crystal ball without the glass -
Your colour, your radiance, the future minus the past...

My prayers, my heart, the unconditional refrain -
Your infancy, your childhood, the team Sommer game...
My openness, my liberalism, the judgements begin -
Your black, your white, your Jewish roots within ...

My optimism, my first aid kit, the sharpener to my mind -
Your beauty, your grace, the "Big Momma" watch no more to wind ...
My adoration, my besotted, the magical child of my being -
Your spirituality, your depth, the Judaism no longer appealing...

My God may He protect you, may He keep you safe from harm -
Your God may He lovingly release you, within the kiss of His outstretched arm...
My adult child, my passion, the warmth of my message to you -
Your life, your time to live it, freedom beckons yes, tis true!

Chloë - Chai -18 - so proud your adulthood has more than just begun
And outstanding spiritual choices - am truly blessed to be your ever loving mum ....

CUCCECHS 11/03/19

I walked from Finchley Central to London Zoo
And bonded with the animals while smelling their poo...
Snakes have no ears but sense vibration in the ground
Young venom knives slit your shit out without a sound...

The parasitic Varroa mite is bad news for honey bees
But what can we do to halt the knife gang culture faeces?
Faron Alex Paul, prefers to walk forward like the Socorro dove
Life is just excrement, too late when you are a dead angel above...

The superb fruit dove's wings whistle when they fly
But no conscience bell rings when youths are wasted and die...
The shape of a bird's beak is closely linked to the food it eats
Stop and search every poor black number two till it retreats....

Only 200 Philippine crocodiles left in the wild
Will the knife deuce carry away your precious dark or white child?
Where can you drown out drill and dare refuse to compete?
Humans wrestling with Komodo dragons for money manure or meat?

Bush trade playing out in the wild west of London and the UK
Faecal matter low lives encourage babies to kill instead of play
Mexican red kneed bird eating spiders becoming extinct
We must cut the crap and love whether we are wealthy or skint...

Only 25 Hainan gibbons left to reach the ground standing up
We all touch Satan's dung when we lose another human pup...
Female birds, more camouflaged to protect their eggs and chicks
Are stabbed to death just the same by the shites with a paltry dick...

Lord Paul of Marylebone's daughter Ambika 4 forever more
Radiant spirit of the Children's Zoo, the poop, the goats and the boar...
Red squirrels few and far, overpowered by the grey
Fine for tigers to discharge life if a predator comes their way...

The invertebrates are spineless and the shit life throws at you smells
Blue bottle flies, good for gangrenous wounds, time the healer tells...
Invisible eye lash mites clean the discharge and really do exist
And we, beautiful minority vertebrates can ditch the knife and the fist...

Lyndon Davis, 18

Aron Walker, 18

Letwaan Griffiths, 18

Jay Sewell, 18

Connor Brown, 18

Katrina Makunova, 17

Louis-Ryan Menezes, 17

Jamie Brown, 17

Jodie Chesney

Nedim Bilgin, 17

Malcolm Mide-Madariola, 17

Abdi Ali, 17

Sidali Mohamed, 16

Danny Gee-Jamieson, 16

Abdullah Muhammad, 18

Ogunjobi, 16

Jordan Douherty, 15

Keelan Wilson, 15

Jay Hughes, 15

Tashaun Aird, 15

Hazrat Umar, 18

Jaden Moodie, 14

Israel Ogunsola, 18

Tomi Salami, 18

DEBT 27/05/08

This world is made of plastic
Though paper trails grow on trees...
Borrowing can be elastic
Till debt brings you to your knees.

We pay for nothing to tell a story
Whatever happened to that accountant Jackanory?
Debt is so hungry, its appetite is so large -
It buries you alive in its pay back charge...

Do you play Faustus or are you the victim?
Sober drunk now or stuck in the rut dictum?
Smell that flower and appreciate the trees -
Don't cut them down to print out your fees....

What we want is what we need
And heinous banks have encouraged our greed.
Till you are scared - life as you know it can no longer wait.
Suicide beckons cos you have passed the final reminder date...

DOCTORS & NURSES, BLESSINGS OR CURSES 02/09/04

Doctors and nurses, blessings or Curses -
Governments bleeding their budget purses ...
Trendy illnesses not quite pristine.
Obesity is our modern cat walk queen.

Isolated and judged is our single parent of today.
If you dare have no partner, keep casual sex at bay,
Should you choose to be a little different?
Allow your child to be more than the percentile weigh
Do you have the courage of your own conviction?
You must by projective default **rue the day!**

I have always loved the rainbow
Be that exception to the rule
Spontaneous decisions
You are no one's fool…

And in the face of prejudice
You still parent and get things done.
Keep your sense of pride and satisfaction
When your child's love is no iconocalastic pun,,,

Poem Continued Overleaf

There is always that glimmering fleck of hope
The atheist smile of God is still there.
Just learn to cuddle your rainbow
Even though it is made up of hot air…

Positive reinforcement like Gingerbread
Real and faithful friends for you…
Keat's logic makes it beautiful
And your mind's eye will make it come true…

GOSH, DOSH!
ROYAL FREE, SPENDING SPREE…
OAK LANE CLINIC
CYNIC MIMIC…

Do children always need saving?
What if their needs are already met?
When bureaucracy challenges happiness
Selfish self-doubt could fester-and yet….

Jobs for the lads, labelling on offer
The real tragedies slip through
While someone is lining their coffer…

Life is too short not to pay heed…
Special need? or nanny state special greed?

EFFERVESCENCE 27/05/08

Darling Fabienne
Thank you for
Accompanying me
On my spectacular
Journey

Thank you
For your faith
And Christianity

Thank you
For believing
In me

Thank you
For saving Me

Thank you
For never
Tiring of me

Thank you
For hours
Of splendid
Conversation

Thank you
For your
Friendship
And confidence

Thank you
For the fun
And the joy

Thank you
For letting
Me into
Your family

Thank you
For sharing
My one and only
Pain of love - Chloë ...

Thank you
For caring
And daring....

Thank you
For life's memories
Captured fondly

Whether abroad
Or next door
Thank you
For your integrity pure ....

Thank you
For always believing
In the good of mankind
When others have forgotten
This to find ....

Thank you
For Seeing Eye to eye
With me
And hugging
Our spiritual deity...

Thank you
For your intelligence
And devotion
In the midst
Of my human commotion

Thank you
For your love
And thank you
For our God above ....

We are stronger
For our differences
When we hold hands
To recognise our mutual senses ....

Thank you my darling friend
For not letting me
Go round the self-destructive bend.

FIBROADENOMAS 21/06/17

Three year old's mum
Finds breast lump
On the loo
Feeling numb …

Spa weekend
Thrown in the air-
Pregnant friend
About to abort
Just isn't there…

NHS sans farce or folly
Scans to pinpoint lucky, jolly
Staple gun core biopsies
Trolley in - bruised anxieties....
Squeezed mammograms are around
To the silent deafening sound ....

Two lumpectomies
NHS freebies-
Buy one get one free!
Expensive breast grocery surgery ....

11 o'clock and 1 o'clock positions
10 minute confused pre op omissions
Failure of coherent registrar
To drown out ambiguous consultant ha ha

Sutures and beads knotted for show
Baby sitters who didn't say no …
Love you forever Nicole and Gen
The family of friends - just say when …

Little Alice in wonderland
Peering through bathroom lock
Mummy's beaded breast
Silly nurse was not a shock!

Private visits once again
So much more pleasant,
Quick and humane ….

17 years old now
6 months parenting to go -
On the home run
For adult child not to know

Just faith, lust
And a tiny little lump
Of fibrous dust…

FIFTY FOR FIFTY 17/01/19

27 Jan, 1969 - baby girl's olive, birth venture
Aquarian's emotional, spiritual adventure
Innately attractive, grasping baby Natalie
Popped out of the pain in the pale, doughnut belly...
Left to play as a toddler with a green glass bottle
Daddy didn't notice the sliced red, ulnar artery wrist model...

Elsewhere, time circles Wolfgang Amadeus Mozart
German opera composed at 11, his genius, emerald, exacting art
Left through the vivid waves to hang out with Marie Antoinette
Ghost of autism and depression floating through our energetic Life net

1979, compound femur fracture for my 10 year old soul
Left to traction, copper healing and reading Lewis Carroll
Circling the author, photographer and mathematician
I escape with Alice to learn my life's lesson and mission
He may stutter round and round with dyslexia and autism
I catch death, upright in bed - schisms of racism and anti-Semitism...

Mohammed Al Fayed the deluded,
Hungry would be "Chairman",
Breathes in 1989
But he never gropes my Tory breasts with £50 notes divine
British in Israel, I throw him back my 20 year old ball
Of food control
And we, worlds apart flutter long lashes into space's black hole

Poem
Continued
Overleaf

1999, not yet pregnant with mixed race sap, yellow green child
30 years beckons, childish attributes - bright, meek and mild
Dictates the explosion of pregnant, round, infectious personality
Raised eyebrows, fluorescent, copper abdomen,
Chloë the tadpole inside me...
Baryshnikov - someone else's Misha, dances the ballet,
Best of all time
As I embrace my "raison d'etre" life decisions full of smiling,
Crimeless grime…

Limo in the snow, magical for a 9 year old Chloë
2009, snakes and ladders hit the ice of my money
Thomas Willis cannot break through the anatomy of my brain
I wonder if he would have thought the round flow of blood
There sane…

And now - wooohoo! Poet and artist supreme
I am catapulting into the journey of 2019
Frank Miller can keep the icon of comic book writer
If I can turn 50, exhibit and publish my "storyism" fighter
50 for 50 - that is what I am aiming for
In the dartboard of my life's artistic score....

FOOTFALL 01/10/90

Prick my wound with the cruel world balm
Then kiss me better with sellotape calm
Caress me with an oxymoron fable
But don't grope or rape me at your table....

Sell me God in your aphrodisiac solutions
But can't and won't buy your omnipresent pollution
Save the multi-faceted icons for the rain
Pluck and suck my beauty from being sane...

Footfall cascading in my mountain of tears
Alcoholism blurred in drunken fears....

GEE WHIZ IT IS WHAT IT IS 01/11/08

Gee whiz
It is
What it is...

South African
Uber babe
Intoxicated serial snatcher
Of life/love blood's knave

Kabbalistic hand
Raises Nelson Mandela's
Imprisoned for white rand...

Worthy of note
His murderous freedom fighting
For the black vote

Yet vaguely unappealing
Is the current corruption
Causing bloodshed in political dealing

Death by your fat
Bodies burnt by your tyres
Choose African National Congress
Or Inkatha Freedom Party
Over white Chaucer lyres...

Although birth right by descent
Not my fight
To pay my rent

Apartheid
Snide
Cowardly hide
No free lunch or ride

Pluralistic in my attitude
Leave me out of violence pursued -
Wow such a beautiful landscape
Full of rape and black children's future
At stake....

Winnie Mandela
Could abuse you
If you let her...

Chip frying heavy on her shoulder
Hand defiant growing older
Wrinkled, gnarled and creased
Is the mantra for peace?

Gee whiz
South Africa
Just is what it is...

GRENFELL TOWER 13/07/17

Grenfell Tower
Shameful shower of fire ....
Corbyn and May
Extra-long incendiary
Polisocyanurate ...
Enough to make you irate -
Ideal and unprecedented
Emotionally burnt and demented ...
Political insulation ....
Socialist fire ... In our nation

Conspiracy theories
Stoked by ignition -
Human bodies
Charred beyond recognition ...
£214 million in reserve funds
Out of reach to grieving mothers and
Sons …

An 8.7 million refurbishment
Much to the incredulous concernment
Of the innocent, multicultural tenants
Will the guilty parties escape penance?
Enquiry - red tape - any heads to roll
Over the climbing black soul death toll?

Greedy bargains
Extortionate pains
To extinguish regulations
Into flammable human remains ....

The milk of community kindness
Could not quench
The heinous mindedness
Of money's stench

Thanks to dirty deals
And politics
There is more to corrupt us
And divide us
Than unite us

HUMAN CONFLICT 11/10/17

"Mental Health Oh Mental health"
Striptease of populist, political slogan
Dangle disaster over poverty or wealth?
Exposed tragedy of the hidden Elitist Trojan

Outpouring of our human eternal conflict
Emotional suicide-worthless, hopeless, helpless
Trinity of self-destruction or pep talk of survival?
Perpetual pain versus pain relief-
Shrink tricked or to predict?

She will be forever young -
She will be forever beautiful-
She lies in the hot Israeli dust
And carry her daily in my heart I must!

Pure and pretty
Funny and witty,
Truly religious
Abandoned by fear and pity....

I will love you now
I will love you tomorrow
But my hands are tied
My lips sealed in your sorrow....

The fishing players live on
Their lives are resumed
But no more "mummy"
Till Messiah has you exhumed....

Did you catapult over
Life's point of no return
When the two men sea ran dry
And the pills embrace you did churn?

Were you scared to be me
On your own and fancy free?
We will never know
And my insanity will never let you go....

ZUMBA was your life, sparkly heels
Death you did not fear it...
Dance then with everlasting Zion's soldiers
In glittery spirit
Lipstick angel -1 did paint you twice
With all my magic
But your fait accompli suicide leaves
Me behind manic and tragic....

HUMAN RIGHTS WRONG HUMANS 24/11/06

Universal respect for each and every
Individual
Yet modernity turned on its head to
Feed liberal residual
Once translated to protect from
Abkhan to Zulus
Hyena human rights lawyers now get
To pick and choose

And butchered UN Campaigners-
Guillotined Paris 1948-
To bury any common sense in the
"Human rights state"
Freedom of expression should of
Course belong to Jordan
But sling home terrorists when we are
Bored of them!

Sierra Leone - harsh conditions in
Prisons and jails
But Israel criticized when
Self-preservation prevails!
Afghanistan governs with illegal
Militias
Pakistan harbours Bin Laden in its
Military compound of pleasures

Bring human rights violations to the
Perpetrators of Haiti
But stop housing terrorists like
Abu Hamza - repeal the treaty!
Stop the recruitment of child soldiers
In Cameroon
And accept intifada fighters are not
About to swoon....

Human rights wrong humans-so
Please let's call it a day
When the guilty are molly cuddled
And the innocent have to pay
Let's apply common sense and build
That bloody fence quick
When your neighbour's out to get
You with his suicide belt death wish
For a prick!

INNER HAPPINESS 22/06/07

Sadness always leads me eventually to smile,
After embracing my unique pain for a while...
Then accept the universality of my struggle -
Adult child and your projective identification in a cuddle…

Are we at inner peace when we laugh or is it when we cry?
Do we let our emotions talk - dare they sigh and even fly?
Rarity is the parchment of our deviant personality.
And is it ever ok to let your guard down on regularity?

Bullies must get shot at with their own personality.
Split lovers in one mind may face their own duality...
Bubble versus trouble, mind-set theatre of the double
Do you know any one marching for peace in Kabul?

Boycott of your own emotions -
Lord save me from prejudice and commotion!
Love and loss, torture and pain
All ultimately help to keep you sane...

Inner happiness must be in your child
Even if the false prophets drove you wild...
Watch her sleep and be at peace -
Gratitude is the best release.

JEW 17/10/19 - EPIC POEM

Rampant, reckless, headstrong and compulsive Nisan spring ram,
Jewish Aries horn caught up in who the hell I am
Isaac's sensational escape from Houdini's life to self-sacrifice
Impetuous Reuven, promiscuous fire and first born vice

Miriam, clap your tambourine, Ruth Bader Ginsburg's not a liar
Dynamism and court justice, your ancestral daughter is on fire
Pesach sacrificial lamb and no more blood libels for Jews
Replaced by the unacceptable face of capitalism in the news?

Resistant to change, raging viral, the inflexible, unyielding Iyar IDF bull
Shake your Taurus horn at Bernard Lee Madoff and the gentile Ponzi scheme pull
Golda Meir, 4th president, teacher, stateswoman and kibbutznik
How do you feel about your fraudulent sons and dirty money in the nick?

Karl Marx, German philosopher, economist and Hebrew social revolutionary
Be the muse for Sigmund Freud, founder of Zion's worldwide psychoanalysis illusory
Should we forget to be humble cos Golda maintains us Jews are not that great?
Or, should we bathe in the kosher Garden of Eden within the Torah's dictate?

Yom Haatzmaut, a day in the life of the spiritual world and independence
Intifada's smoke screen burns those who choose to sit on the fence
Shimon, your cloak, cattle killing, mummy hated, angry temper, dagger Jew
Nonetheless, my protective brother, I salute, love and look up to you

Sivan, open the earth to apikores, jealous Korach and feed your Gemini twins
Rebellion born and died with David – who dares blaspheme never wins
Levites are leaders, not shepherds, gate keepers, choir singers in the Temple
Deborah, prophetess, warrior bride, actually judged so rightfully judgemental

Anne Frank, German born diarist and fairy air sign victim of the Holocaust
Martyred for being an Israelite, beautiful ghost servant of the Pentecost
Resourceful life stolen, my eternal honey-child, teenage Jew
Wrapped in Torah, your Semitic debut haunts eternal for me and you

Golden calf, tablets broken, misfit hedge fund crab lives to crawl another day
Samuel Israel 111, suicide faker, money taker, integral part of anti-Semitic cabaret
Come save the day martyr's daughter, Talmudic scholar, ethnic Beruriah
And kingship rid cancer's fast of Tamuz, roar for us once again Yehudah!

Poem Continued Overleaf

Immorality or love, you chose to lie with Tamar
And admit her righteousness over you by far
Your signet, staff and bracelets not gone to Timbuktu
Reclaimed lion cub to lion, Jesus died for who?

Moses leader of the Israelites who saw God face to face
In the kiss of a rock cleft Aharon pursued peace and grace
Both died in Av, twice special houses of God demolished/gone
Babylonian Nebuchadnezzar and Roman Titus long since forgotten

And yet, Jew and gentile can't help but touch the wall
Proselyte in your midst join us so we don't fall
Tu Be'Av grape harvest, can you see it Kabbalist Ha'ari?
White dressed maidens in the full moon – was one of them me?

Lion Leo, one of the four Fire Rivers representing the fixed sign tyre
Gave birth to Issachar, suckling mummy's mandrakes and sexual desire?
A strong ass for the Torah? Shekelesh sea people? Are you a man for hire?
Or precious spiritual reward donkey for your brother, float my sins up higher?

Edna Ferber, American novelist and playwright "Che Sera Sera"
From bin to 10,000 copies sold, thank mum for Dawn O'Hara
Enthusiasm, drive to express self and endless faith for the review
Biblical heart is that enough to escape the Holocaust queue?

Virgo's purity lost in the creation of mankind's world
Moses ascends for the stone tablets, our history is unfurled
Practicality and caution, slichot our first aid kit here on earth
Baby Leah Gottlieb prefers to tell you what her swimwear is worth

Elul calls for practicality, caution and support your brother's first family
Zebulun entrepreneurial, import export Judaism for sale by the sea
And yet can we dwell within that name and pull off a Jewish coup?
Or, Maxwell to Green pension pots, greedy Jew means sue, sue sue….

Abraham, Isaac and Jacob our forefathers all born and judged in good favour
Jewish New Year, Fast well and Tabernacles, add Gedaliah for ethnic flavour
Tishrei Air sign, conceptualisation, socialisation, communication
Libra, come snap us up in our traditional chicken soup adoration

Annie Leibovitz, photographer of celebrities like naked John Lennon
Curled in foetal position with Yoko Ono two hours before he went up to heaven
Orange type 5th stone Leshem Dan from Bilhah our photo's bijou
Messiah's mother's snake won't strangle my life's poisoned tattoo

Poem Continued Overleaf

Thirsty for water the ark set sail to drown out the flood
And now we drench Noah's rainbow in freshly spilt fluorescent blood
Scorpio – are you resistant to change? Inflexible and dynamic
Or Trotsky's Marxist theories – do they set mankind into panic?

Cheshvan, Rachel's tomb in Bethlehem, favourite one, who does she save with her tears?
Ofra Haza's grave Manuka voice reminds me of AIDS related pneumonia fears and endears
Garden of Eden, fixed water sign with fatal river flu
Can you flow empathy, life divine and chance anew?

Naphtali, did Rachel wrestle with Leah over the consequence of you?
Beautiful words versus fertility, for barren Rachel is this in lieu?
Inferior status, the benign breast lump of fibrous tissue
Integral to the description of what it is to be a harmless Jew?

Maccabees, bows and arrows arch present for the first five days of Chanukah
Zeida's cooking spoon violin, Yiddish theatre passed over in a Holocaust survivor
Sagittarius rainbow of colour, little black dress designed by tailor's son Ted Baker
Too fat to fit, I sing, dance and act along to Pearl Harbour's Bette Midler

Gad, warrior born and died to become Leah's troop this month
Zilpah, mistress or concubine, war and peace for Tolstoy's grunth?
Illegitimate yearning for spiritual development, fire in a stew
Borderline east Jordan Jew, still part of my Kislev crew

Ezra the scribe and Maimonides, Jewish physician and philosopher
Both died in these thirty days so that we can hail them as our own scholar
The writer returned the Babylonian exiles ready or not to Jerusalem
The astronomer brought Mishna Torah to the universal Muslim

Anthony Stuart Fastow, born Capricorn criminal and businessman
Glad I misspelt your name you antithesis of Uncle Sam!
Fast of Tevet and Jesus, can you bleat his sin out and atone for us all
Babylonian siege, goat of a false prophet - wipe out his ill-gotten haul

Ernestine Rose, suffragette and doubter of modern orthodoxy
Inherited from your mum and won, proud to be your proxy
Practicality and caution, millennia of material earth spent through
Tarshish happy amber stone, olive trees and good reputation Asher for you

Poem Continued Overleaf

Bob Marley, was your paternal grandmother Jewish?
Reggae, Rastafarian, Aquarian, your lyrics never shrewish
Hero and icon, exodus preacher and pirate rabbi
Kabbalistic secrets in your songs for us all to buy

Powerful and stubborn, let's break the old boundaries
Erratic air sign, solitary cruise liner in the Garden of Eden please
Neil Diamond and Carol King, for the sake of your Jewish souls sing
So we abuse victims can stop extreme eating or dieting...

Joseph onyx stone, righteous equerry, Hebrew father to Ephraim and Menashe
Your boastful self-denying artistic offspring Samuel Menashe with his panache
Scribe art, storyism, take on life for the desperate poet laureate
Natalie Sommer, never betrayed Jesus to the San Hedrin like Judas Iscariot

Shevat, ecological holiday and Jewish New Year for all fruit of the tree
Seder for Rabbi Yitzchak Luria of Safed, four cups of wine but not for me
Intellectual and powerful, I am not into the joys of voodoo
Kindness is not a weakness, better that than be smug, successful you

Back to Moses born and died on the 7th Adar
So that the sea of Torah nourishes fish and Jews near and far
Charles Ponzi was an Italian swindler and petty con artist
Copycat Jews the emulating Chilul Hashem cancer in our midst

Pisces, integrity, sincerity, empathy and piety
Sarah Schenirer first orthodox feminist with sobriety
From the Belz and Ger Rebbe, encouragement vocal
Educated girls still left segregated, covered up in total

Rashi first to print Hebrew commentary on the Old Testament
First port of water call for ships and Jews to spiritually ferment
Ben Oni, son of Rachel's affliction or fortuitous Binyamin
Renamed by Jacob, life measured by life and death and sin

Framed and scapegoated for stealing a golden goblet and cup
Do we let ourselves down when in this world we eat our merits up?
Ravenous wolf Mordechai would not compromise or make do
And Purim
Is the living legacy of what it means to be a Jew

KETCHUP 24/12/18

Hokkien "ke-tsiap", fermented fish sauce
Fragrant ketchup or the perimenopause?
Female chilli powder mood swung hoarse
Tears greeting Xmas nutmeg and Santa Claus

Brown sugar and cinnamon, voluptuous bottle
Sex and caresses for her, oestrogen full throttle
Passion, hugs and kisses "dans la nuit" of youthful prime
Night sweats, untouched breasts, frigid insomnia for mine

Squeezing the bottle of her youth, motherhood paused
Squares and diagonals of red hot love we once caused
Before age and pain - the trapeze artist and acrobat
Stopped me concentrating, and made me forget and fat

LOST IN CLARITY 27/09/18

She chose to swap my token bracelet of love and Kol Nidrei
For celebratory dinner with and infinity necklace from Tré
I am conflicted; somewhat torn and addicted to my faith
Equally love my daughter, her boyfriend and what God saith..

Where is the bikini beauty secular and free as a bird?
Her sunbathed Judaism shaken - her soul never stirred...
Pomegranate - come and impregnate me with your seed
So that my mitzvot, yetzer tov and motherhood can succeed..

MAGICAL MUSICAL NOSTALGIC ZEDAKAH (CHARITY) 02/01/18

Never sell your Judaism short as you whizz through your life
Sometimes chew the genteel cud of kindness to combat pain and strife....
Always grateful to a place of holiness and history that has saved my very soul
Kinloss you devoured my nomad, secular, irreligious despondency whole....

Bette Davis, Judy Garland, Phyllis Nathan Benevolent Trust and Deanna Durbin
Dance the Hora jive in my mind to the beat of the womaniser Jeremy Corbyn ....
My heart is full of love my psyche bursts with Chasidish memories to the brim -
Modern Orthodoxy you are my Egyptian Exodus from meaningless life on a whim....

Eleven years of Shabbat joy and happiness spent passionately with Kinloss' beautiful children
My one mitzvah of hope and love enveloped in the blessing of charity within our brethren
Thank you Kinloss and Rabbis for having the faith to let charity set my history free
And some kind soul, continue to bless and support - simply put please buy me!

MEAT AND MARRIAGE 17/05/17

It only happens when I married you -
Lipo husband you made my dreams come true -
Meat and marriage forever can melt into one
72 year old septuagenarian and 47 year old bride fun!

It only happens when I married you -
True love and artistic wisdom can shine through -
With 600 closest friends to feel the karma that day
And 60 bridesmaids and page boys to do it our way!

It only happens when I married you -
The who's who of Rabbis on our side too -?
We are so lucky to have such family and friends
And faith in God - the magic that transcends!

It only happens when I married you -
Gratitude eternal for doing all that you do -
To make my life worth one for the living
And let emotional respite do the giving!

It only happens when I married you -
Something borrowed, something blue -
Berketex bride in a Cinderella dress
Beautiful moments to treasure with no redress!

It only happens when I married you -
You adore me and you always knew -
That "never in a million years"
I under the canopy and you in tears!

It only happens when I married you -
Fluorescent canvas - cameras, action CUE -
Poetic license and passion to form a queue
As you break the glass to say I do, I do, I do!

It only happens when I married you -
Mutual companionship for us two -
The destruction of the Temple we never forget
Or the 17 year old boy who slipped through the net!

NUDE WITH ATTITUDE 05/09/17

Is it rude not to be a prude?
Modesty dictates to me seem crude ....
Vulgar is the Jewish princess' honour without a voice
Forced to keep her body under wraps for society's choice

Rabbi Yosef Karo - 16th century
Not for me perhaps the codification sentry....
"Do not draw close to her nakedness" makes sense
But my elbows, knees and collarbones are not your fence ...

Stilettoes, nails and uncovered hair will always be there
Hugging bright colours to avoid depression's glare
Love of being Jewish won't alter my mood
Cos I just love being nude with attitude....

O GOD 17/12/18

O - god - if you were an academic
I would reject the endemic
Copycats in "Disobedience"
They could not have mocked your credence...

O god - If you were a bank robber
I just wouldn't bloody bother
To shoot the "Old man with a gun"
Why begin the end before death has begun?

O god - If you were benevolent
I would not be hesitant
To snuggle independent Scrooge's "White XMAS"
Out of SNP's salmon breakfast of loch ness....

O god - if you were a paracetamol
I would readily swallow Labour béchamel
Circles of carbs and "Wonder Man"
Food control tossed away in the can...

O god - if you were a line
I would digest, never gag on mine
Manometry's metre of "Spiderman"
Muscle of Conservative love in the stomach van

O god - if you had a heart
I wouldn't mentally leak or fart
Green for go the extra "Green Mile"
Gentle giant martyred for social democrat bile

O god - If you knew toilet humour
I would be your IBS rumour
Bloated waste of "Ladykillers"
To prop the purse of your actor pillars

O god - if you were a colour
I would paint you not just for pound or dollar
O god the words would live straight, wavy, supreme
Artist and poet laureate - could I dare to dream?

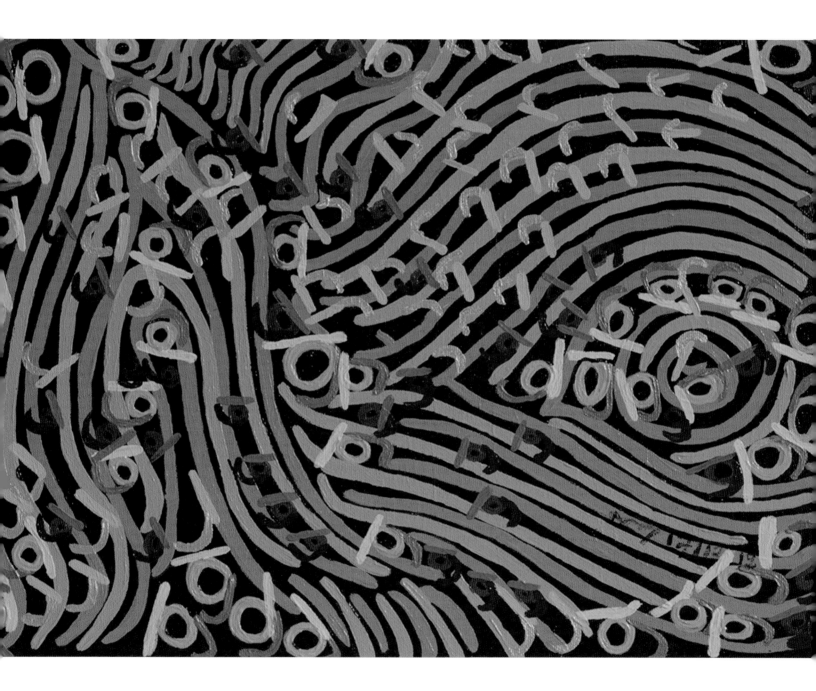

OUR VERY SPECIAL FRIEND GEORGE 28/03/19

We are so honoured, privileged and humbled George
For the 16 years of friendship and chats we did happily forge
Over tea, and just the one "little tipple" (or two) you would say...
Your friends and family celebrate your life and achievements today

We treasured your stories as a war child evacuee
And you taught Chloë so much from when she was three
Your integrity and resilience such a lesson for us all
Your tireless work ethic - no job ever too big or small

An intensely private, reserved man with no time for fuss
Yet you made our lives so special by giving time to us...
We relived your soldier experiences and your love of the steam train
We travelled the world of memories in that brilliant brain, again and again

We will cherish you always, never forgetting every XMAS Eve
When you would indulge a little with us and gifts would receive
We will raise a toast to you each 17th July, your birthday
Fish and chip tea, sponge cake and my paintings would come your way

Successfully rejecting the idea of modern technology
You never had a mobile telephone or wasted time on a TV
Your spare time was invested in fishing, then painting
You loved the roses, reading and knowledge acquainting

We will look fondly at your photo on our computer table
Your chair picture on our wine rack, part of your life's fable
You loved your train driver dad, your mum and all the family
We thank all your loved ones, part of your beautiful living legacy

Now your star can shine over Norfolk, Archway and Kentish Town
Places of interest for you, rest in peace without a care or a frown
We release you to your loved ones, God bless you we say
Reunited with your mum and dad and sisters Winne, Joan, Doris and May..

PAS TOI, PAS MOI, PAS MAL 19/07/18

Pas toi, pas moi, pas mal
Not my blood, birth banal
Someone else's raw grief
You're passing with no wreath…

Pause to reflect
Memories to deflect…
Erased from compunction
Psalms to mask the dysfunction…

Gin and tonic
Alcohol logic
Love and breeze
You fail to breathe…

Yet, you were there
Perhaps you didn't care…
Au revoir, adieu
Melancholy bleu….

Where are the spirits
Called up without limits?
You said they would not go
Are you now Jew to follow?

Rest in peace le Maroc
No feelings or tears ad hoc
I cannot adapt or sway
There is no connection today….

Love will set you free
And keep the predators from me…

PESACH 11/04/19

Beautiful, mystical, heavenly blue
My cut off soul, reincarnated ultramarine Jew
Climbing His spiritual ladder of coerulium healing
In the presence of God, 50 - doing my cleaning....

Roll back the Seder, hospital bed at 10 - no others
God brought me out to reject my no show Rabbi Brothers
Black nurse embraced me - freed from Babylonian inclusion
"Just tell me what to sing!" I loved her Wedgewood effusion...

The four questions fluorescent in His image divine
We bonded with grape juice, David's offspring and mankind...
Stories of Frogs and lice, wild animals and Pestilence
Boils, locusts, darkness, life lessons of pain and resilience....

Grape juice at hand, 20 year old outcast rejected again
Emmanuel's last supper, God saved me in the cobalt verge of sane...
"Just tell us what to sing!" there is no need for conversion
My mistress "secularity" still steers me clear of Exodus Persian...

In my 30's I am a Hebrew - the wine goes happily in
Motherhood means purpose, so Greek secrets out and I win
Cups of tea, jugs or the light blue Haggadic pitcher
Plurality of my Creator with redemption in the picture...

The Romans would have my tribal woman of 40 years' past
But forefathers and mothers' traditions abound so we may last
The symbolic sacrifice of the loss of the firstborn
Lamb to man is crucified - God took me back torn and worn....

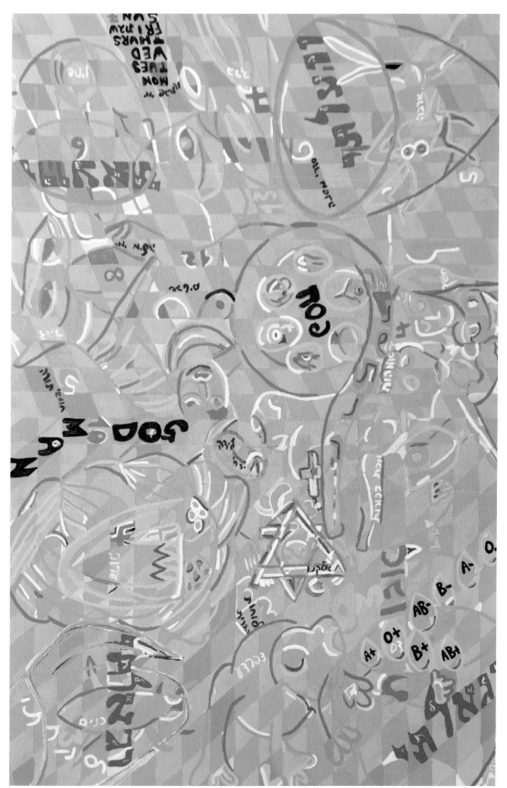

QUEER 09/10/18

God's inclusive image,
Non-welcoming and "Queer"
Equates to religion's debate
And division of fear…

God spun an "affectionate regard" angle
From the "religious" dust of the ground
Did he breathe in or out our bone and flesh?
Without a godly "sexual" sound?

God blew "judgement" and part of HIS soul
Into the male, calculus "lonely" nose's hole
One of his sides God filled with female, vibrant flesh
Oedipus complex swapped, clinging to "wife" mesh

God created plus signs
When He created HIMSELF
He created "HIM" male and female
And left lesbianity on the shelf…

Poem Continued Overleaf

God whether heterosexual, transitory or situational
Divided us with no "penetration whatsoever anal"....
Sexual orientation may not be forbidden
Just any "drop" of procreational male semen...

God knitted homosexual divergence
With poetic David singing of its resurgence...
'Thy love to me Jonathan was wonderful"
Greater than my women's loveless earful....

God's Jewish Christian image Jesus
Whose sexuality is clearly ambiguous...
Preferred to die rather than transgress
Would not have been crucified today for wearing a dress...

Jesus loved his mother and 200 years later was proclaimed divine
As a man he loved Mary Magdalene was she a possible concubine?

Laws applying to men naturally should apply to women too
But child bearing Leah was hated by them not by you...
Rachel once barren, her absolute righteous value cries for us all
Spot the Spodik wearing LGBT transvestite - see her tears fall?

Chanukiah flames of hate, their blood is upon them
Jealous that woman from man can only create mayhem..
Aliyah, minyan, Torah blessing and witness
Talmud Torah versus political correctness...

RUB HER OUT AND DON'T LET HER PLAY YOU AGAIN 20/07/17

My pencil of life pauses to reminisce
As I sharpen the mind's eye
I want to rub out my unconditional love ....

Tears before bedtime
Mine
But it is not about you
They say ....
Away from the Sabbath Candles

18 lovechild-chai
Erased as I CRY....
She was my life's icon
Now a woman, she has gone...

Sex, politics and religion
Lies between us with division....
Unconditional love
Can never
Rub her out
But don't let her play you again....

95

Whisky pure -
Dandelions' cure,
Love's Allure?
Melancholy cure -

Fetish of old -
Masturbate cold!
Rhapsody told
My heat is sold
On you!

SUKKOT 05/05/19

I am the one in a million good deeds bankrupt Pharisee
Sukkot does not taste Torah or smell oral law for me
Citron pump bleeds hooker's green rabbinic tradition
Strangles the oral law into brilliant yellow Sadducee submission

Genesis; sukkah crawl of ancestral patriarchs and the 12 tribes
My gender fluid "ushpizin" visit my canvass with concubines and wives
The myrtle looks into my soul - it smells good but has no taste
Did the disciples ditch the Torah for humanity? What a waste....

Numerology; permanent green light of God's people and Exodus
The skeleton spine has no active merits, its Torah palm is obstreperous
The love affair with corruption puts paid to the Hasmonean dynasty
And we are left with a wall and Hoshana Rabah's chance of amnesty

Leviticus; "Hashem's special tent" and "Hashem's special house"
No torah deeds - just vacant kisses on the lips for the willow spouse
Harder than taking up the four species - the brain's "Arba Minim"
Without rules and regulations does faith have the same meaning?

Numbers; clouds and manna could protect Israelites in the desert
Now, crooked garden hut is exposed to wind Jew hate alert
Diagonals and lines, past present and future already defined
And earth, air, fire and water is all just in your mind

Deuteronomy; Moses' last speech and eloquent repetition
I embrace my identity with iridescent white recognition
Simchat Torah means presentations and analytical phonetics
And we dance our brown souls into mixed race genetics...

SUSPENSION OF DISBELIEF 30/07/09

"Suspension of disbelief" -
What can it bring but ultimate grief?
In the real world Peter Pan
Where you don't quite make the mark of man…

And if those genes
Never came into play?
Happy clappy Helen of Troy
Spit out your son's DNA!

Ecstatically cruel,
Just a little morbidly unkind…
Getting on with your life -
You happily left my child behind…

Sinister satisfaction -
Black denial must rule -
So morose poker faced jokers -
Is it cool playing the fool?

Giant Tinker Bell is forced to float away
So you can martyr her for not forcing him to stay -
And do you rue now what you always knew was true?
That you should believe in your fairy
Cos she looks so much like you!

THE ELATION OF DISCRIMINATION 27/03/09

My puppet show mind
Mimes to the elation of your discrimination...
I am inept-
Can't fathom your sign language

Race locked
In deaf/dumb emotion...
My persecution
Cannot dissolve yours -
You won't melt mine.
So I tingle truth
While you chime time...

Incoherent rants,
Your succinct overture
To my bias.

Status quo of unmatched minds...
You are as deep as a flat note
And I don't want to sing it-
So I dream of harmony
And cross out duality -
Fall into my pride
As you are buried in yours -
And blink reprise
Kiss my Semitic intermission ...

Bacterial infection
And yeast
Breed, bleed and beget us ...
Free choice
Yup - your own pessary
To pessimism ...

I choose to scratch
My E.coli and fly ...

THE PERFECT PARENT IS CHILDLESS 30/08/08

The perfect parent is childless - wait and see
Till love and experience kill off patience for me!

From Jesus to Schneerson to Mother Theresa -
Atheist, observant or non-believer…

Hypothetical parent is so much easier
Than high temperature parenting
With anxiety the omniscient ring leader...

TORN TENDON 18/02/19

Gold and silver supraspinatus tear shouts out "let me be seen!"
8 months prior to the Consultant's diagnosis on 20 December 2017
Too deaf to anything but the addictive endorphin workout
I paid my trainer to break me and watch her disappear at the fallout

My pale pink blood may never flow again to the attic room at the inn
Shoulder forlorn, strenuous activity, elbow push ups are in the bin
Couldn't do my bra, my biceps tendon garden gate is off its hinge
She shies scared of my rotator cuff injury, should I legally dare to whinge..

Two guided injections later, post pale blue bursitis and frozen shoulder
I swapped warrior definition for love of parchment and getting older
My shape is even more beautiful because I am kind, alive and free
Conscience clear to walk and climb, restores life's balance for me

TOXIC RELATIONSHIPS 19/06/18

My scarlet letter baby
Is my adult child's black albatross
Gift from God, my life's love
Gained via financial loss.
My sweetie man's progeny are
A deceitful, cheating curse,
Vultures and parasites, man's poison
At its vicious, twisted worst

I gave my every penny
To my innocent daughter
But I never threw money
At a problem - no soul slaughter

My sweetie man gave you every penny
And taught you the ABC -
He cries - why did you exploit
And steal my lifespan from me?

Toxic relationships know
No boundaries
Tear up the address book
And throw away the key
Don't bother with justifications
Or legacy pleasantries

No entry signs for truth's names,
Frogs' venom reigns supreme
Negative karma and control games
Sibling love is not what it may seem....

UTOPIAN ATTITUDE 20/11/18

Yesteryear I love Rahab, Jericho's prostitute
For hiding Salmon and his mate so resolute
Flax stalks of barley for all to see on her roof
King of Jericho, collateral damage the proof

"Our lives for your lives"!
The men assured her
And she rightly survives
Over to Joshua - Israelite daughter

House of David, our Boaz meet your regal mum
Innkeeper, booty hills and chaste the 3 days' sum
My heart forever melted, in responsible, educator gratitude
Yours dissolved in fear, but roar lioness for never being a prude…

Today, I don't get Rahab's lost youths allowed to climb
And won't turn a blind eye to vandalism and crime
The roof of our precious house of God and prayer
Not to feather the nest of entitlement layer by layer

Dinosaur, playing king and queen for this life's day
Our beloved, bored God's children I will never betray
Thank you for the opportunity to hang in there and serve
Asteroid may kiss you farewell, for that is what you deserve…

My objective plain and simple is just to get the job done
Life without control and good deeds is the antithesis of fun
So, on reflection I am proud to embrace my utopian attitude
If that means credit for me as visionary and zero balance for you as rude!

111

VACUUM 06/01/19

We don't live in a vacuum
But my mind resides in its safe room
Optimism there kisses, would never assume
Negative thoughts knocking, weaving their loom…

Split and noisy my hoover brain fume
Depression dances over the blue psyche womb
Giving birth to hide and seek doom and gloom....

Brown falls, earth's winter a locked, lonely tomb
Spirituality reigns in the void of my head's moon
Green anxiety and jealousy eager for sun's bloom
Royal priesthood - immortality beckons for whom?

I believe in one God in my busy chatroom
But idle money idol goes zoom, zoom, zoom....
God's angel Satan falls forward, farting feather air plume
Rich dangles out of reach - so poor, abundant plucking I presume?

Plus personality, minus one mad, mood witch on her broom
Fire-fighting empiricism, sceptical philosophy died with Hume
No matter the pressure, black space always must resume
And can't swallow the water of their side in my life's classroom

WELCOME BABY ARTHUR HEDGEHOG GODSON 27/03/18

Welcome baby Arthur Hedgehog Godson
We wait for you, boisterous and blessed with fun
You are not contained, wriggling in our arms just yet
But my Love commissioned, has painted you before we have met

Calmly snoring for my paints, my precious and beautiful one...
Dream on, sleep tight till life wakes you - Eliza and Kevin's firstborn son
Trinity of parenthood and child, Jesus loves you meek and mild
Your godmother Natalie -
Pluralistic, Jewish and forever free

I pray life keeps you safe and sound and clear
Of the wrong sort of pain anywhere, far or near
I pray life makes and blesses you warm and kind
Just like your parents - their treasure of love for you only to find

Your history Artus, knights of the Round Table
Worldwide courage little bear, of that you are able -
Resilience of stone, regal as a king
Free from any prejudice let your tiny heart always sing

Be happy and content with your family hedgehog unit
Spare your spikes and sleep at night so as not to ever ruin it!
We love you little boy, as we gently rock you back to the land of Nod
And give our thanks to man-child's precious gift from God

WOBBLE 06/02/19

While walking off
Borderline high blood pressure
And cholesterol
Obnoxious eyed
Obscure,
Kissed my £500
From the hole in the wall...
Bank balance bled -
Blind vision,
Sophisticated crime
No one can see
Beyond the cold -
Fraud winks,
A stroke against
One in four
And innocent me!
Limerick scammers
Who splash out on contempt
For kindness and mankind
Eel of Satan
Will wobble your slate
And hell makes it easy
For you to find....

X-IT-BREXIT 04/12/18

Brexit remains to be seen
On 29 March 2019…
May borrow, beg or steal
Gifting Corbyn - socialist zeal…

Brexiteer and/or Remainer
All unite to fight against her…
3 historic Commons defeats
Chanukah's oil anointing cheats..

Rebels and little grey men
Last rites for uncertainty's amen…
Sanchez limps up to the altar
In an EU attempt to sacrifice Gibraltar…

Foster twists the Minority knife
Treacherous kiss from the DUPI
Union Jack, May could lose your life
In the EU pirate's backstop - Irish Sea…

Juncker resembles Fagin
"Got to pick a pocket or two"
May's flat tune of 39 billion
NHS porkies for me and you…

Blair can preen
With the budget queen
Second referendum
Nonsense momentum…

Boris and Farage
Collateral pay back charge
Cameron the toff and the twit
May mean no hard or soft Brexit

I am one of the 17,410,742
Who voted to leave the bully EU
And now the toys are out of the cot
X it Brexit could cost us Brits a lot

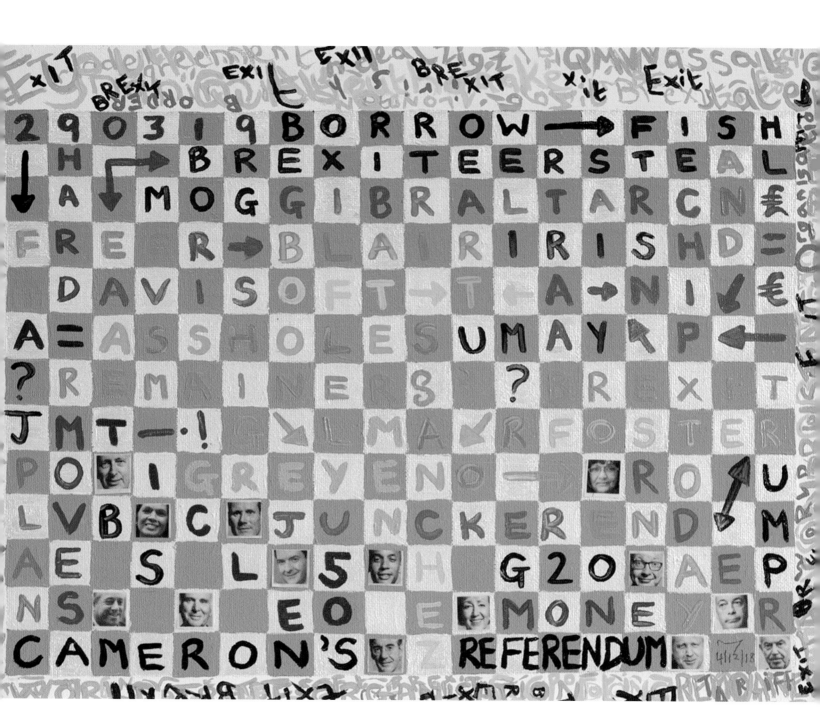

YASMIN 07/01/19

She surprised me with the beauty of her face
Against all odds we shared our different race
Honorary Jew my tiny, model Christian child
Safe with friendship shielding families wild....

19 years old and pregnant in the breeze
30 years old and somewhat eager to please
Play centre with dirty mats smelling of cheese
Toddlers and mummies met without emotional striptease....

United in our love for our children
Sky of memories pinpointed in our devotion....
Absent present daddy putting out fires without her boy
Absent ghost daddy's girl shipwrecking her mum ahoy....

She found the grandmother who didn't want to know
And took my baby out so my pain didn't show
Doctors and nurses, blessings and curses
Shouldering life together, dead baby sister in hearses...

Love where the material god of money dissipates
And safe from the pain of misplaced family resonates
Precious tears proudly owned and faithfully owed
As we articulated our experiences and stories unfold...

I was kinder the age she was when we first met
And worked for her parents, didn't know it yet
Ehlers Danlos and post orthostatic tachycardia syndrome
Coursing through the blood to make its unwanted home....

Upstanding and wellbeing is what I pray for her
Peace of mind and hurt be gone, not allowed to stir
I love you sweetie just as you do me
And pray your mind sets your spirit free....

YOM KIPPUR! 03/10/09

Outpouring of words and sentiment...
Penitent prayer-that annual time
To whisper religious ethnic precedent
Into Rabbinical flavoured rhyme...

Wailing Wall, peace process always to stall?
And fist to breast-victims of terror, continue to fall?
Peace to Jerusalem, repentance for us all
Embrace multiculturalism, do we have the gall?

Do we feel judgement?
Without or within?
Are we in God's image?
Or do we encapsulate sin?

Love and hate, religion, strawberries and cream....
Pale to dark blood brothers, can we all live the dream?
Universal common brotherhood always wails,
And one day they won't hate us - God's forgiveness prevails...

Ram's horn, born to blast Semites today,
Alarm bell to kiss those who choose to pray....

ZEALOUS LECHER 09/09/90

Zealous lecher beckons me
But who is really climbing
That finger pointing
Passive aggressive liar tree?

Neediness, night and day
Messages bombarded my way
Stay away, nasty man
Punch your own bloody fist
Don't want to be your sacrifice - hugged or kissed!

You protesteth far
2 near and much
My married man
Just can't help it but touch
"Soft spot for you", tick tock....
Next victim for your self-esteem clock

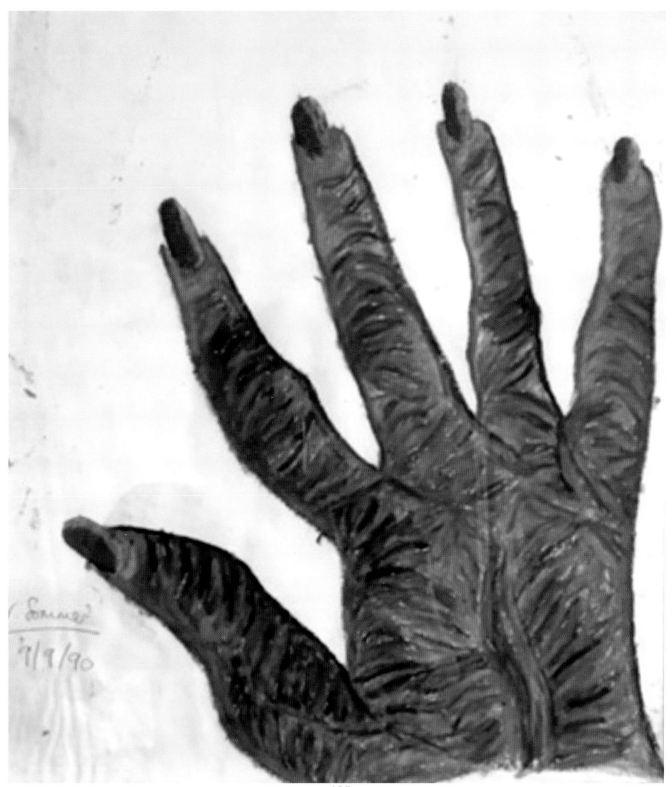

Sommer
7/7/90

125

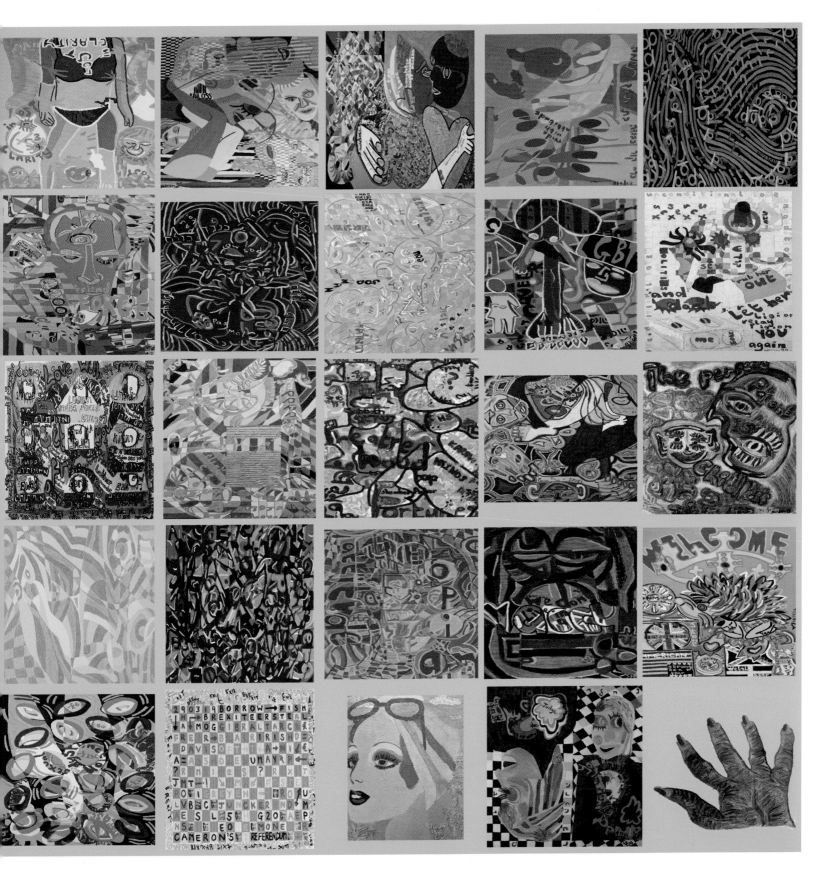